IS EASTER IN THE BIBLE?

BY: BRITTANI RAMIREZ
@2024 SCRIBBLES and SCRIPTURES

scribblesandscriptures.com

"Is Easter in the Bible?"
I wondered aloud one day,

As signs of church events
for Easter came into play.

EASTER
SUNDAY SERVICE
10AM

"Why celebrate Easter, is it
something we should do?"

My parents sighed softly and said,
"We can discuss this with you."

"In the Bible, my child,
Easter's story you will not find,

It's a mix of traditions,
of a very different kind."

BIBLE

"Yah gave us feasts,
for remembrance and reflection,

Not for bunnies, eggs,
and its springtime connection."

"Yah's feasts are sacred,
with meanings deep and true,

Not like Easter's customs,
which we don't pursue."

"Easter comes from old times,
a tale not so divine,

Named after Eostre,
a claimed goddess of ancient design.

A festival for spring,
but not from Yah's command,

A human-made celebration,
spread across the land."

EASTER SALE
Easter   Sale

Easter's origins are steeped in old pagan
lore, Not aligned with Yah's divine
command.

This celebration holds traditions and
symbols galore,
Yet none shall mark or guide our hand.

Men claim its for The Messiah
for His crucifixion and His rise.

Yet Yah, in His wisdom so wide,
Gave us Passover, a feast to forever
be between our eyes!

This human-crafted tradition,
Breeds sinfulness within.

It fosters material idolatry,
And the covetous urge to win.

"That's why, dear child,
we don't embrace this day,

We follow Yah's true feasts,
in a faithful way.

In His wisdom and love,
our hearts find their rest,

In His appointed times,
we feel truly blessed."

GLOSSARY

Messiah: The anointed one promised in the Hebrew Scriptures to deliver and redeem the people.

Man-made Event: An occasion or celebration originating from human tradition rather than directly from Scripture.

Easter: A religious man-made observance commemorating the resurrection of The Messiah, traditionally celebrated on the Sunday following the first full moon after the vernal equinox.

Pagan Practices: Rituals and worship practices not found in the Bible, often associated with polytheism or idol worship.

Elohim: A Hebrew term used in the Bible to refer to God, characterized by a plural form to denote majesty or sovereignty.

Eostre: A figure or deity associated with spring and fertility in pre-Christian traditions, often discussed in the context of the origins of the name "Easter."

Idolatry: The practice of venerating or worshiping idols, images, or representations, considered a violation of the commandments in biblical teachings.

Coveting: The intense desire for the possessions, qualities, or status of others, deemed inappropriate or sinful according to biblical commandments.

Divine: Of, relating to, or characteristic of God or a deity; heavenly, holy, or sacred in nature.

YHWH'S FEASTS

Spring Feasts:
Passover (Pesach)
Feast of Unleavened Bread (Chag HaMatzot)
Feast of Firstfruits (Yom HaBikkurim)
Feast of Weeks or Pentecost (Shavuot)

Fall Feasts:
Feast of Trumpets (Yom Teruah)
Day of Atonement (Yom Kippur)
Feast of Tabernacles or Booths (Sukkot)

DID YOU KNOW
that each of these Biblical feasts represents our Messiah, and foreshadowed His coming? Here's how :

Passover (He is our Passover Lamb)
Unleavened Bread (Represents His sinless life
Feast of First fruits (His resurrection)
Pentecost (Holy Spirit given to the disciples)
Feast of Trumpets (His second coming)
Day of Atonement (atonement through The Messiah)
Feast of Tabernacles (He will dwell with us during His reign)

SUPPORTING SCRIPTURES

- ## Mark 7:6-9

Jesus said, "Isaiah was right when he prophesied about you hypocrites; as it is written: 'These people honor me with their lips, but their hearts are far from me. They worship me in vain; their teachings are merely human rules.' You have let go of the commands of God and are holding on to human traditions."

- ## 2 Corinthians 6:17

Therefore come out from among them And be separate, says YHWH. Do not touch what is unclean, and I will receive you."

- ## Deuteronomy 12:30-31

"Take heed to thyself that thou be not snared by following them, after that they be destroyed from before thee; and that thou enquire not after their gods, saying, How did these nations serve their gods? even so will I do likewise. Thou shalt not do so unto YHWH thy God: for every abomination to YHWH, which he hateth, have they done unto their gods..."

Jeremiah 10:2-5

"Thus says the Lord: 'Learn not the way of the nations, nor be dismayed at the signs of the heavens because the nations are dismayed at them, for the customs of the peoples are vanity...'"

PRAYERS

- ## Prayer for Gratitude:

"Dear Elohim, Thank You for my family and my friends, For the love that we share and that never ends. Help me to be kind, to share, and to play, To cherish our moments, each and every day. In Your loving care, I am never alone, And I'm grateful for the blessings You have shown. Amen."

- ## Prayer for Peace:

"Elohim, Fill my heart with peace and contentment true, Help me find joy in the things I do. Though around me, others may celebrate with cheer, Let me remember, Your presence is always near. May I be a light for others to see, The peace that comes from You, not from a tree. Amen."

- ## Prayer for Generosity and Love:

"Father in Heaven, Teach me to give, not just to receive, To open my heart, and in You, believe. Help me to share, to be someone's light, Especially for those who might be alone tonight. May my actions reflect Your love and grace, And bring a smile to another's face. Amen."